ETIQUETTE AT SCHOOL

KATHERINE YAUN

NEW YORK

Published in 2017 by The Rosen Publishing Group, Inc.
29 East 21st Street, New York, NY 10010

Library of Congress Cataloging-in-Publication Data

Names: Yaun, Katherine, author.
Title: Etiquette at school / Katherine Yaun.
Description: First edition. | New York, NY: Rosen Publishing, 2017. | Series: Etiquette rules! | Includes bibliographical references and index.
Identifiers: LCCN 2016029588 | ISBN 9781499464788 (library bound) | 9781499464764 (pbk.) | ISBN 9781499464771 (6-pack)
Subjects: LCSH: Student etiquette—Juvenile literature.
Classification: LCC BJ1857.S75 Y38 2017 | DDC 395.5--dc23
LC record available at https://lccn.loc.gov/2016029588

Manufactured in China

CONTENTS

INTRODUCTION

You are sitting in the school library, trying to finish work on a big paper due that very day. Your top priority is to finish and submit your homework. All of a sudden, a classmate walks by and says, "Hey, how are you?" You look up but are so stressed and absorbed in your papers and laptop that you barely mutter a greeting. Talking to your friend is not your top priority.

Still, you are pretty close, and figure she probably saw how flustered you seemed and will give you a pass. A couple of days later, you pass by your friend at her locker and say hello. She greets you back, but it is a bit cold and unenthusiastic. What happened?

In this case, etiquette should have guided you to return your friend's greeting—"Hi! I'm fine, thanks!"—even though your circumstances are not ideal for conversation. You can then politely let her know that you are working on an assignment that is due soon, and ask if you can chat with her later. Your friend had the same teacher once and surely would have understood the pressure you were under. But the entire experience was hopefully a reminder that just a little bit of etiquette can go a long way.

Whether your circumstances are ideal or not at any given time, making sure to follow basic etiquette can cement friendships; make things run smoothly with fellow students, teachers, and administrators; and maintain harmony. Etiquette is often situational. That is, different situations call for different responses to those around you. But following rules of etiquette fosters a general aura of politeness and respect among people.

Etiquette guides people in how to act in different settings: at parties, at school, on dates, while shopping, when

Quiet collaboration and independent work are the most common rules of etiquette in the school library. Socializing is better to do in open spaces like in the hallway or outside.

traveling, and when visiting friends, to name just a few. These situations are more orderly and harmonious when everyone uses basic etiquette and manners.

Mastering the social graces at school will also help prepare you for many situations in which proper etiquette is required in the world at large, whether it is in higher education and academia (college, university, and grad school) or in the working world. It also helps build the foundation for smooth relationships and socializing among neighbors and in civic society

In this book, we will explore how etiquette forms a framework for interaction at school. This is true whether we are talking about smaller environments such as the classroom; larger ones such as the auditorium, gym class, or the school cafeteria; or even groups of students congregating outside during a lunch hour or after school. It is also valuable to know how to behave in extracurricular school settings, including clubs and teams and at school events, and how to negotiate the modern and increasingly important terrain of social media.

CHAPTER ONE

GETTING FAMILIAR WITH SCHOOL ETIQUETTE

Many of the lessons you learn at school go beyond academics: they are also social, cultural, and personal. Learning the basic etiquette appropriate to various school settings will help you maintain smooth relationships now with your friends, classmates, and teachers. It will also aid you later in life whether you are at work, at home, or socializing. Etiquette smooths some of the rough edges of school interaction during a time when many students are just learning the ropes.

ORIGINS OF ETIQUETTE

The term "etiquette" comes from the eighteenth-century French word *étiquette*, meaning "prescribed behavior." In France around the seventeenth and eighteenth centuries, there was an established set of procedures expected of people in the royal court, the social headquarters of kings, queens, and other aristocrats. Ordinary citizens like soldiers and merchants received little cards, or "etiquettes," with instructions on how to behave. These directions included properly bowing to those of higher social rank. People who were skilled in proper etiquette made better impressions and excelled in social climbing.

Similarly, there is a hierarchy of authority at school. Students are at the bottom. Above them are teachers and school administrators. Principals are the top managers at school, overseeing the work of teachers and administrators. Students arrange themselves, too, both officially and unofficially. A captain of a team might be higher in the social

While there is a hierarchy of authority at school, all people deserve respect. Whether you are interacting with teachers or classmates, etiquette can help you figure out how to act.

hierarchy than a student who is introverted and keeps to herself. Popular kids often wield more social capital. Older, more experienced students tend to have a higher social status than new students. It is important to note that people at all levels are required to respect one another, no matter what their roles or informal positions are.

WHY WE NEED ETIQUETTE AT SCHOOL

Etiquette is necessary at school because this is a place where people are constantly collaborating. Students come together for many reasons—to learn, to work on a homework project together, to play a sport in gym or on a team, or to produce a musical. It is human nature to consider yourself first, and competition and differences can make tensions and resentments flare up. Etiquette tempers these tendencies and ensures that people take into account others' needs and feelings.

Consider how you would behave if you encountered your best friend in math class, then your math teacher outside of class, and your social media rival outside of school on a field trip. Just like the French word suggests, etiquette can instruct you and can make the answers to these questions very clear: nod or smile an acknowledged greeting to your friend in math class but try not to talk too much while class is in progress; say hello to your teacher in the hallway in a respectful way; keep a safe distance from your social media rival if you feel that you cannot be near him or her without arguing. These instructions are about extending respect, politeness, and kindness in a way that is appropriate for the person and the place—or simply avoiding potentially negative situations in favor of getting along.

MORE THAN JUST SCHOOL RULES

School is known for rules. However, etiquette is the unwritten set of rules and expectations for politeness and kindness, including the processes by which we maintain them. While related to etiquette, school rules like the following are not the same thing as etiquette:

- **No running in the hallways.**
- **Bringing a doctor's note to excuse your absence when you are sick.**
- **No skipping class.**

These three rules are policies that a school has created to ensure everyone is safe and gets the best education possible. Yet the first example, no running in the hallways, is also related to etiquette because if you had others' best interests in mind, you would avoid speeding down a crowded hallway and causing injury to others. Similarly, the rules on doctors' notes and skipping class are also rooted in etiquette because they are ways to show you respect your teachers, even if they are also requirements for you to fulfill if you are absent from school or class.

Etiquette is not simply an invention to impose constricting rules on young people. Rather, it solves and prevents problems. In meaningful and genuine ways, etiquette is about making other people feel comfortable, safe, valued, considered, and respected.

SCHOOL RULES, MANNERS, AND ETIQUETTE: WHAT'S THE DIFFERENCE?

The words "etiquette", "manners," and "rules" are often confused. Even though they all relate to managing behavior in different settings, there is actually a clear difference among these terms.

Manners are general behavioral guidelines and may include prescriptive orders like "show respect to your teachers, principals, and classmates." Saying "please" when making a

Etiquette solves and prevents problems. For example, wearing a school uniform can create a sense of equality among students from diverse backgrounds.

request, "thank you" when you receive a gift, or "Excuse me!" when you bump into someone are examples of proper etiquette. The latter are the mechanisms by which you show respect and courtesy, or demonstrate those good manners.

Etiquette covers more specific codes of behavior. For example, it is good manners to show respect to your teacher but good etiquette provides you with specific ways to demonstrate respect. If your theater teacher's name is Mark Smith, you should call him Mr. Smith rather than Mark. When Mr. Smith gives you an instruction, you can nod to show that you are listening, or even say, "Yes, sir."

Rules are policies and procedures that people in a position of authority create. While often rooted in etiquette and a desire to make sure everyone feels respected, rules are also rooted in other motivations such as safety or adhering to schedules and budgets.

THE BENEFITS OF ETIQUETTE

The benefits of etiquette are numerous. It fosters respect and communication among you and your teachers, friends, and classmates. Etiquette helps manage and prevent tensions and makes relationships easier.

In many jobs and professions, rudeness can set you back or even get you fired. On the other hand, your genuine ability to act in a respectful and courteous way can elevate your status among work colleagues and bring about promotions and raises. This last point is particularly important to remember when you are a student in school. If you want to succeed both now and later in your professional life, etiquette is key to your success.

CHAPTER TWO

ETIQUETTE IN COMMON AREAS

Modern schools run the gamut from small ones in remote areas to large schools in cities and suburbs with thousands of students. No matter what the size of your school's campus or student population, it is obvious that slightly different behaviors are appropriate and expected in different school venues: the classroom, auditorium, gym, library, hallways, and other places.

COMMON AREAS OF SCHOOL

Change can be hard, and the slightly different expectations and rules that you encounter as you get older can also take some getting used to. This is true when you leave elementary school and enter junior high, and then again move from junior high to high school. These environments are all significantly different than your home. School settings all have similar etiquette rules, though there are always slight variations among them.

Wherever you learn, you will be around lots of students, whether in the classroom with a few dozen classmates or with hundreds more in common areas. You will also encounter

In a crowded hallway, it is fine to let loose and joke around with friends between classes, but make note of the direction foot traffic is flowing to prevent accidents.

teachers, school administrators, and visitors at school. When you put all these people and places together you get a dynamic environment. Etiquette is more formal and polite around school officials and teachers in indoor academic settings. In outdoor or social settings with friends and teammates, etiquette is more informal and relaxed.

THE AUDITORIUM

Auditoriums can be formal or informal depending on the type of event. At a school assembly, it is acceptable to relax and chat beforehand. But once the event has begun, common etiquette is to be quiet and listen to someone who is speaking, regardless of whether it is a fellow student, a teacher or administrator, or the principal. While anyone on stage deserves your respect and attention, this is especially true of visiting speakers. Your behavior, individually and collectively, reflects well or poorly on your entire school community. You should feel some amount of regret if a speaker leaves believing your student body to be rude or unruly. Make sure to clap at the end of any speaker's words, too.

Avoid taking video or photos in situations that demand more gravity, or seriousness—for example, during a serious assembly about a school issue or problem, a memorial service for a member of the school community, or similar situations. If you need to leave for a bathroom break or any other reason, wait for a pause, such as a transition or break in the assembly, or exit during applause.

It is customary to avoid eating while an assembly is under way. If you do have a drink or beverage, avoid canned beverages that make that disruptive crack and hiss when they are opened. When you leave, or when the assembly is over, it is impolite to leave your garbage behind. Take your empty containers to a garbage can or recycling bin. As in the classroom, do not put your feet up on the auditorium chairs in front of you. Besides potentially disturbing your classmates in that row, it is disrespectful to those on stage.

IN THE CAFETERIA

Food and socializing go hand in hand, and the cafeteria is a more informal and relaxed environment than the classroom.

Schools tend to have many different social cliques, divided in different ways. It is polite and kind to include others who may be sitting alone, especially new students who have moved from elsewhere or exchange students from other countries who may feel lonely or out of place.

Respect the "first-come, first served" standard when it comes to lining up for food or snacks, even at vending machines. Shoving in line or standing too close on someone's heels are also no-no's. Move along at a steady rate in line. Ideally, if the food line is self-serve, and

The cafeteria is one of the most informal and relaxed environments at school where you can take a break from studying to eat and chat with friends.

someone is taking the time to help themselves, you can move ahead of them if you ask permission.

A well-mannered student treats teachers and fellow students with respect, but also cafeteria workers. Food servers and cooks are your elders and deserve a "please" and "thank you," much as you would utter it at the dinner table at home. Accidents and spills sometimes happen, but

EXCHANGE STUDENTS

Exchange students are high school students from other countries who have chosen to live in North America for a year or two in order to attend school, improve their English, live with a host family, and learn about American or Canadian culture.

Make exchange students feel welcome. Ask them if they have any questions, and invite them to hang out. It will enhance your own understanding of the world to learn about other cultures and places. It is also the kind thing to do.

Part of new students' acclimation is learning about the social mores and standards of their new environment. It might be slightly different in their nation or culture of origin. Such students should be given leeway when it comes to etiquette rules or rituals with which they are less familiar. Students familiar with the majority culture should also take time to learn about the etiquette and rules of exchange students or students from immigrant families. This way, they will be less likely to treat them differently and will hopefully learn cultural tolerance in the meantime.

avoid horsing around and creating a disgusting mess that workers or janitorial staff must then clean up.

Many school administrators have imposed newer rules on their students' cafeteria behavior, especially when it comes to noise. It is natural to want to socialize and let loose after hours of the more strict behavior enforced in classrooms. But it is in everyone's interest that you keep shouting and raised voices to a minimum. Dozens of students' yells and screams echoing through an enclosed space can be highly disruptive.

Most students come to the library to study or do homework. Out of respect for these efforts, it is best to keep nonessential talking to a minimum in the library.

THE LIBRARY: A QUIET AND CONTEMPLATIVE SPACE

The best etiquette in a library is to be quiet and focused, though this is starting to change. If you use any kind of media while studying, the key is to use headphones for smartphones, tablets, laptops, and other electronics. Keep nonessential verbalizing to a minimum, because the library is not a lunchroom or an auditorium.

THE GYM

Physical education and school sports are their own self-contained worlds within the larger school setting. The dress code is different, as are the activities. These spaces are among the remaining ones where real competition is encouraged. They are also ones where differences in ability and appearance might cause tensions.

Overweight or clumsier kids may feel alienated, as may children with disabilities or health issues. Students should avoid using language around their peers—namely, those that do not perform as well in physical activities—that shames or alienates them. They should also make an effort to be inclusive in games and sports, especially where students themselves make the rules and manage the games. Everyone should be given an opportunity to play and do their best and, above all, to have fun.

MYTHS AND FACTS

MYTH: School and public libraries are places to meet up and socialize.

FACT: Visitors to both public and school libraries may be louder than in earlier eras. But the library is still a place where the rights of your fellow students or citizens to read or study in peace should come before loud talking and other disruptive behaviors.

MYTH: The etiquette at school never changes.

FACT: In the 1950s, every teacher was referred to as "Sir" or "Ma'am" and when they entered the classroom, everyone stood up and unanimously said, "Good morning." Now the start of class is less formal for many students.

MYTH: The need for etiquette doesn't extend beyond school property.

FACT: Since the overwhelming majority of young people connect with each other, and even teachers and administrators and other members of the school community, it is important to be polite, mindful, and extend the same courtesies to fellow students online as you would in person.

CHAPTER THREE

ETIQUETTE IN THE CLASSROOM

Classrooms are the center of any school, and the most structured settings in them. Class rules, guidelines, and schedules for students to follow contribute to this structure. There are rules in class that you will get in trouble for breaking. But there are also standards of etiquette that make classroom activities run more smoothly and ensure that everyone, including teachers and students, feels respected and valued.

PUNCTUALITY

Arrive to class on time, Arriving on time shows respect for your teacher and your classmates. Students who stroll into class five or ten minutes late create disruptions. These can break fellow students' concentration on a problem, drill, or reading exercise or interrupt the teacher's lessons. If you get there early, you actually have time to socialize or goof around before the teacher is ready to start the lesson. Then it's time to quiet down, get your materials out, and be ready to concentrate on schoolwork.

The classroom is one of the most structured environments at school, one where participation is prized. Raise your hand to show your teacher you are curious and interested in the material.

MATERIALS, SHARING, AND BORROWING

When a school loans out textbooks and other learning materials, proper etiquette dictates that you should return these as you received them, without marking them up or defacing them. Think of the others who will have to use them later. Similarly, it is customary to clean up after yourself after completing an activity or project. A student who doesn't clean his or her desk or workspace can make for a distracting or disruptive environment.

GIVING CREDIT WHERE CREDIT IS DUE

When writing essays, be careful not to pass someone else's ideas off as your own. Not only is this bad etiquette, as you are robbing them of the credit and praise for their idea, but it is also plagiarism, one of the highest academic offences you can commit. Be sure to give credit where it is due in the form of proper citations. Consult your school librarian, teacher, or internet resources for the proper citations for all kinds of sources.

Another time to give credit and work equitably is when you collaborate on group projects or with a partner at school. If you have several people on one project, you can divide up tasks accordingly. Often, someone will be interested in research, another perhaps in writing, while another classmate may be best suited to share data or results in a classroom presentation. Learning to work together is as important as the actual research a group engages in.

Examples of poor etiquette in group work or when working with a partner include those who hog all the work, and the credit. Classmates will resent such a person, and they will do their best to avoid him or her in the future.

Another example is people who do not carry their weight or do their share of the work. They are content to sit by and let others do the heavy lifting. They are resented, too, because they took advantage of the hard work the other group members did to earn the good grade.

Consider also the things you must keep well stocked for yourself, like paper, pens, markers, and other school supplies. Make sure to keep track of these, ensuring that you have enough week to week. No one wants to be the person who is constantly borrowing other people's things. If you truly lack resources, arrange to meet with your teacher in private to discuss how to solve the problem.

BE ATTENTIVE AND PARTICIPATE

Texting in class or whispering with friends are two of the ways that students might violate classroom rules and etiquette. An adult in the workplace who behaves similarly might get reprimanded or even fired. The social contract in the classroom is that the teacher teaches, while students, when not participating, pay attention. This means keeping eye contact with your teacher and also doing the same when you are having a classroom discussion with another student.

Avoid behavior that is distracting to others, such as being a class clown. This is someone who is more interested in entertaining classmates than making sure everyone gets the most out of class time.

Participating is important, both to make lessons engaging and to show teachers you are curious and interested in the material. Try to give everyone a chance, however, as the loudest voices and highest hands can sometimes drown out more introverted classmates. Naturally, you should always raise your hand to answer a question, and invite others to share what they think. Do not shout out answers. In most classrooms, a teacher will not acknowledge shouted out responses, and will only call on those who have their hands up.

Grades are important but they are not everything. If you or a classmate gets a bad grade, do not dwell on it. Instead think positively, learn from any mistakes, and move on.

"WHAT DID YOU GET?"

Grades are the most common means of evaluating students. Good grades are important, but they are not everything. It may be tempting to reveal your grades to others, but it is best to tread carefully. If you are a high achiever, it is sometimes okay to compare grades with another. But doing so with a larger group of classmates, or the whole class, verges on bragging and should be avoided.

Studying in a small group can help everyone learn in a more relaxed environment. It can help you focus more on the assignment's central ideas rather than on grades.

SPEAKING IN CLASS

Whether you are listening to a teachers' lecture, another student's presentation, or a guest speaker, the best etiquette to is actively listen and then engage with the speaker in dialogue when invited to do so. It is rude to whisper, use your cell phone, or look out the window when someone is speaking in front of the class. It takes courage to stand before a group of people and speak, and the speaker deserves your attention and respect. When you are the one presenting in class, you would also want everyone's attention. Speak clearly and confidently so that others can hear your good ideas.

TEN QUESTIONS TO ASK A SENIOR ABOUT ETIQUETTE

If you need some help in figuring out the best etiquette around school, ask an older student who knows the ropes. Here is a list of questions you could ask:

1. When you first started school, did you automatically know what good etiquette was, or did you have to learn it?
2. How did you learn etiquette?
3. What was one embarrassing mistake you made when it came to etiquette?
4. Who pointed out your mistake(s), a classmate or a teacher?
5. What mistakes in etiquette on a school campus should I avoid?
6. Why do you (or don't you) follow the rules on a school campus?
7. Why do you think etiquette is important at school?
8. If you could change three rules at school what would they be and why?
9. What rule of etiquette do you consider old-fashioned or outdated?
10. When was a time that etiquette was a handy tool for you at school?

CHAPTER FOUR

ETIQUETTE AT SCHOOL EVENTS

Some school events are formal and serious, while others are informal and relaxed. Certain events take place on school grounds, either during the school day or after hours. Field trips, sports and academic team competitions, school plays and musicals, fund-raisers, and many other gatherings may take place somewhere off school grounds.

SPORTS AND ACADEMIC COMPETITIONS

Team sports such as football, soccer, basketball, baseball, and volleyball bring communities together. For schools competing against each other in the same city or county, you may have fans of both teams supporting their athletes. It is fine to cheer, clap, yell, jump around, and shout out in protest if you disagree with a referee's call.

Your exuberance and support should remain within civilized limits. It is bad etiquette to heckle a visiting team, for example. No matter the competitive spirit among you and your school's students, visiting teams are your guests and demand your respect.

At sports events, fans of opposing teams often sit near each other. When your team is ahead, it is fine to jump and cheer, but keep things within respectful limits.

Team members on the field should practice good sportsmanship. This means keeping your cool when you disagree with a referee or opposing team members. If a teammate or rival team member falls down, extend a hand to help him or her get up. Playing aggressively is fine and often expected. Playing to try and intimidate or even injure other students is wrong and sometimes even verges on criminal behavior.

SPORTS AND NATIONAL ANTHEMS

The national anthem is typically sung before a sporting event begins. It remains common etiquette in many places to stand during the anthem and, in some cases, to put your hand over your heart. The crowd often sings along, or at least mouths the words. This is a good opportunity for both teams' fans to come together and remember that despite team differences, everyone is part of the same community. If you happen to be attending an international sporting event in which you are playing against teams from another country, it is good etiquette to be quiet when the other country's anthem is playing. When their anthem is over, you can clap respectfully. Remember: if you do not feel very patriotic, it is a good idea to stand out of respect to those who do.

The same spirit of hospitality should reign when your school hosts an academic competition team. Greet the visitors and make them feel welcome—this includes student competitors, their family and friends, their teachers and coaches, and the competition's judges. If any of these visitors need help with directions or finding a particular room, lead the way. When your school is hosted by another, then the same is true. You deserve to be treated with respect by your hosts.

At the end of a game, common sportsmanship calls for offering polite congratulations to the winning team—or graciously accepting it if your team is the winner.

ON YOUR BEST BEHAVIOR

Many competitions and field trips require travel. You might go to another school in your area or even somewhere far on an overnight trip. When you stay in a hotel, by all means enjoy the experience and have fun, but be polite and respectful. Simple things like taking turns in the bathroom, keeping all media and noise at a low to moderate volume, and walking rather than running in the hallways show respect to your hotel roommates and to sleeping guests, perhaps even those with young children, in neighboring rooms.

FIELD TRIPS

When you go on a field trip, time is of the essence. First of all, it is important for you to show up ahead of time in order not to keep a busload (or more) of fellow students and others from leaving on time. Be sure to pay whatever fees you need paid up front and have all permission slips filled out. Otherwise, you may not be allowed to go and may have to stay behind at school.

Stick with the group when you are on a field trip. This will help you stay on schedule and get the most out of a guide's presentation.

Once you arrive at your destination, it is important to stick with the group and be mindful and respectful of strangers. Stay close to your teachers, coaches, chaperones, and classmates. Pay attention to the guides, and be respectful and attentive when they are speaking.

If you are at a museum or historical site, keep loud conversation and horseplay to a minimum. Many people visit such sites to unwind and think deeply about history and art, while others are visiting as part of their jobs, or as scholars. Being loud or disruptive is rude and selfish.

PROM ETIQUETTE

Prom has been a tradition for over seventy-five years, and it remains the most important high school dance of senior year. Good prom etiquette is about having respect and consideration for your date and the event. Ask your date out in person at least one month in advance of the actual prom to give him or her enough time to prepare and find the appropriate formal clothing. Girls typically wear long gowns, and boys wear tuxedos, although this tradition is changing. You want to be comfortable but look your best. If you already have a date or prefer to go solo, be honest and direct, but kind, in your response. At the event, be prepared to dance and have a good time but don't drink or do illegal drugs. Pay attention to your date during the prom, and always leave with the person you arrived with.

If you are given the chance to wander around on your own, pay attention to the time and return to the meet-up spot at the designated time. Everyone is on a set schedule when you are on a field trip, and holding up a large group of people and preventing them from returning to school or home on time is truly bad etiquette.

PERFORMANCES

During school performances, proper etiquette requires audiences to be respectful and attentive. Some musical events require quiet attention (such as classical music) while others allow for more rowdy and raucous audience participation, like rock, R&B, hip-hop, or dance performances. Clapping loudly for a friend who has a guitar solo in the school's annual talent show is a way to show her your encouragement and support. Generally speaking, however, being an audience member means being quiet and attentive, putting away your cell phone, enjoying the performance, and holding your applause until the end. This is very similar to the etiquette one should follow with public speaking.

CHAPTER FIVE

NEGOTIATING ETIQUETTE IN AN ERA OF SOCIAL MEDIA

Adhering to proper etiquette in any school setting has never been simple, especially among large groups of young people trying out new things, making and breaking friendships, and generally finding out who they are. Making and keeping friends at school often requires some give and take. Your clothes, appearance, attitude, and interests will affect who you hang out with.

How you treat people, both in person and off campus, is vital. Increasingly, etiquette concerns today extend beyond school, both via in-person interactions and on the all-important social media platforms and apps that dominate the lives of teens and preteens.

SOCIAL MEDIA AT SCHOOL

Snapchat, Facebook, Instagram, Twitter, WhatsApp, Vine, Pinterest, and many other social media applications, or apps, including email and video chat, make up the virtual venues where teens socialize these days. You and your friends likely use one or more apps, or combinations of them, to make

You and your friends likely use one or more apps, or combinations of them, to make plans at school, after school, and on weekends.

plans at school, after school, and on weekends. You likely also communicate with one another, including gossip and rumors, using both messages, photos, and other means.

PRIVACY AND TRANSPARENCY

Modern etiquette on social media requires that we understand the line between private and public. Your social media presence on Facebook and other apps can be private or public. You can send a message directly to a friend that no one else sees, or you can send a message that your friend and her entire social network—sometimes hundreds of people—can see. Only share information and pictures that you know your friend would not mind a big group of people seeing. Otherwise, it is customary that you just message someone privately and directly.

GETTING ALONG ONLINE

Even minor arguments and perceived slights among friends at school can boil over and be amplified by social media posts. Think before you hit send on an overly aggressive text, Facebook comment, or tweet. The impact of the initial message often outweighs your later efforts to walk it back or apologize.

Avoid online blasts that spread rumors or suggestive posts and photos of yourself or friends. Remember that there are negative effects from spreading such content. Even if you delete posts or your digital paper trail, the data stills exists and can be retrieved later in life. The best advice is to try to avoid posting content that may come back to haunt you or your school friends.

BULLYING 24/7

Consider whether you do or say the same thing in person as you would online. This includes behaviors like flame wars, heated arguments that are more about personal attacks than someone really having a discussion on an issue. It also includes piling on and bullying.

Would you be ashamed to call out someone in real life and witness their hurt and shocked expression at your attack in person? Remember that nowadays online attacks can feel as

real as bullying in person. Even worse, modern bullying does not end at the school entrance or schoolyard. It can continue after hours online and can even take place while the victim is logged off, as comments and other electronic messages pile up in their absence. It is bad form to spread rumors and gossip—whatever truth there may be to either—about friends and acquaintances in person, online, or via texting and other means of communication.

Be kind—or at least respectful—when you are online. For the person on the receiving end of an online attack, this can feel as real as bullying in person.

AVOIDING DANGER ONLINE

Your classmates' feelings and privacy are not the only considerations when making decisions about social media content. You also need to consider their safety and your own. Avoid strangers and suspicious profiles, but also make sure your privacy settings are strong. Think twice about sharing info unless you're absolutely sure about the identity and trustworthiness of those with whom you interact online. You don't want to expose yourself, or your friends, to predators or other unscrupulous people, like identity thieves or other criminals.

RESPONSIVENESS

Friends may expect quicker responses to texting and Snapchats. You can generally take a little longer to reply to emails, voicemails, comments, and the like. If you take too long to reply, though, the moment may have passed and your response may seem out of place or ill timed. If you take too long to reply to a text, your friend may think you are ignoring him or her.

However, it is also important to remember that not everyone behaves the same way on social media. Some people are less engaged than others and may prefer in-person

If you are at the movies, the film's action and the people you are with deserve your attention. You do not have to reply to every text immediately.

or phone interaction. Before getting annoyed with someone for not replying right away to a message or a post, think it through. It is good etiquette to give someone breathing room, too, and time to catch up with you. They may be busy with class, a guitar lesson, a basketball game, or any other number of activities. It is bad etiquette, conversely, to constantly follow up for an answer from someone if they have not answered you back. They will do so in their own time, and repetitive questioning or commenting can be annoying or downright harassing.

THE RIGHT TONE

In person, it is easier to tell if someone is joking or serious, happy, angry, or upset. Even talking on the phone, you can make out someone's general attitude or emotional state by their voice. Online or social media messaging and commenting make it somewhat harder to decipher whether someone is joking, mad, enthusiastic, disinterested, or having any other emotional response. While emojis, exclamation points, and other things can add context, even these can be somewhat lacking.

In addition, it is easy to be sarcastic and mocking on social media. Again, this is because it is tougher to see the true consequences of your actions and the pain inflicted on those who are targeted. Always remember the ultimate rule of etiquette and personal interactions in general: do unto others as you would have them do unto you.

aggressive Marked by forceful action or readiness to fight.

breach A break, rupture, or violation of something, including of etiquette.

campus The land, property, and buildings that make up a school.

class clown A student who is more focused on entertaining classmates than on schoolwork

collaborate To work together with one or more people.

conversation Social interaction and exchange of opinions, ideas, or observations.

courtesy Respect for and consideration of others.

etiquette Rules of social behavior in a certain place or situation.

evolve To adapt and change over time.

harmony A sense of calm and calmness in relations among people.

hierarchy The classification of people according to ability or economic, social, or professional standing.

modernize To update and make current in terms of taste, style, or usage.

recreation Time off from work or schoolwork marked by enjoyment, amusement, or fun.

spontaneous Coming from a momentary impulse or natural tendency without external planning or influence.

tact Sensitivity or skill in dealing with awkward or difficult situations.

teacher's pet A student who has won the teacher's special favor, often resented by other students.

versatile Able to embrace a variety of subjects or skills.

FOR MORE INFORMATION

Council of Ministers of Education, Canada (CMEC)
95 St. Clair Ouest/West, Suite/Bureau 1106
Toronto, ON M4V 1N6
Canada
(416) 962-8100
Website: http://cmec.ca
The CMEC is an intergovernmental body founded in 1967 by
    ministers of education to serve as a forum to discuss policy
    issues and a mechanism through which to undertake activities,
    projects, and initiatives in areas of mutual interest.

International Association of Professional Etiquette Consultants
    (IAPO)
167 Midland Place
SE Calgary, AB T2X 1N1
Canada
(888) 322-5621
Website: iapcollege@fabjob.com
The IAPO is a membership association created to provide education
    and business development services for people working as, or
    studying to become, professional etiquette consultants.

International Society of Protocol and Etiquette Professionals
13116 Hutchinson Way, Suite 200
Silver Spring, MD 20906-5947
(301) 946-5265
Website: ispep.org
This society offers the community of protocol, etiquette, and
    interpersonal communications professionals the opportunity to
    network, pursue continuing education, and obtain certifications.

JDW Social Education Programs
1776 South Jackson Street, Suite 1120
Denver, CO 80210

(303) 757-5333
Website https://www.cotillion.com
JDW Cotillions is recognized as an authority in educating young
people in the art of social skills and social dance training.

National Center for Social Education (NCSE)
1776 South Jackson Street, Suite 1120
Denver, CO 80210
(303) 757-5333
Website: https://www.cotillion.com/ncse
The NCSE offers certification in social skills education to
entrepreneurs and others who wish to offer this type of training.
One example is school teachers who wish to instruct classes in
social skills education in schools, for after-school extracurricular
activities, or on an individual basis.

US Department of Education
400 Maryland Avenue SW
Washington, DC 20202
(800) 872-5327
Website: http://www.ed.gov
The Department of Education's mission is to promote student
achievement and preparation for global competitiveness by
fostering educational excellence and ensuring equal access.

WEBSITES

Because of the changing nature of internet links, Rosen
Publishing has developed an online list of websites related to
the subject of this book. This site is updated regularly. Please
use this link to access the list:

http://www.rosenlinks.com/ER/school

FOR FURTHER READING

Bailey, Diane. *Cyber Ethics.* New York, NY: Rosen Publishing, 2008.

Black, Rebecca. *Etiquette for the Socially Savvy Teen: Life Skills for All Situations.* Seattle, WA: CreateSpace Independent Publishing, 2014.

Eberly, Sheryl. *365 Manners Kids Should Know: Games, Activities, and Other Fun Ways to Help Children and Teens Learn Etiquette.* New York, NY: Harmony Publishing, 2011.

Ephron, Delia. *Do I Have to Say Hello? Aunt Delia's Manners Quiz for Kids and Their Grownups.* New York, NY: Blue Rider Press, 2015.

Fine, Debra. *Beyond Texting: The Fine Art of Face-to-Face Communication for Teenagers.* New York, NY: Canon Publishers, 2014.

Fulcher, Roz. *Mind Your Manners!: A Kids Guide to Proper Etiquette.* Mineola, NY: Dover Publications, 2013.

Furgang, Kathy. *Netiquette: A Student's Guide to Digital Etiquette.* New York, NY: Rosen Publishing, 2011.

Hayes, Tina. *Getting Ahead With Etiquette: Roadmap to Success for Young Adults, Teens & College Students.* London, England: Cheemah Publishing, 2013.

Landau, Jennifer. *Cybercitizenship: Online Rights and Responsibilities.* New York, NY: Rosen Publishing, 2014.

Packer, Alex J. *How Rude!: The Teen Guide to Good Manners, Proper Behavior, and Not Grossing People Out.* Golden Valley, MN: Free Spirit Publishing, 2014.

Richa, Joelle. *Guide to Good Manners: From Precious Parents to Precious Kids.* Hobert, NY: Hatherleigh Press, 2015.

Rossi, Patricia. *Everyday Etiquette.* New York, NY: St. Martin's Griffin, 2011.

Ryan, Phillip. *Social Networking.* New York, NY: Rosen Publishing, 2011.

Sonneborn, Liz. *Frequently Asked Questions About Plagiarism.* New York, NY: Rosen Publishing, 2011.

"Classroom Rules of Etiquette." Oprah.com, July 2008. Retrieved February 16, 2016 (http://www.oprah.com/relationships/ Classroom-Etiquette).

"Facts About School Bullies and Bullying Behaviors." *Bullying Statistics: Anti-Bullying Help, Facts, and More.* Retrieved March 8, 2016 (http://www.bullyingstatistics.org/content/ school-bullying.html).

Adams, William Lee. "Switzerland's Last Finishing School." *Time.* November 14, 2011. Retrieved February 16, 2016 (http:// content.time.com/time/magazine/article/0,9171,2097304-2,00 .html).

Department of State. "Host Family Handbook: Promoting Educational and Cultural Exchange." April 1, 2016. Retrieved May 10, 2016 (http://www.nw-services.com/host%20 family%20handbook.pdf).

Harrison, M. A., C. E. Bealing, and J. M. Salley. "2TXT or not 2 TXT: College Students' Reports of When Text Messaging Is a Social Breach." *Social Science Journal,* March 9, 2015.

Institute for International Education. "Open Doors 2015" and "2015 Infographics." November 16, 2015. Retrieved May 1, 2016 (http://www.iie.org/Who-We-Are/News-and-Events/Press- Center/Press-Releases/2015/2015-11-16-Open-Doors-Data).

Knapp, Alex. "Proper Etiquette in The Age of Social Media." Forbes.com, January 8, 2013 (http://www.forbes.com/sites/ alexknapp/2013/01/08/proper-etiquette-in-the-age-of-social- media/#703135ab7c26).

Mazur, E., and Y, Li. Identity and Self-Presentation on Social Networking Web Sites." *Psychology of Popular Media Culture.* American Psychological Association, August 18, 2014. Retrieved May 1, 2016 (http://psycnet.apa.org/ psycinfo/2014-33477-001).

National Center for Education Statistics. "Average Class Size in Public Primary Schools, Middle Schools, High Schools, and Schools with Combined Grades 2011–2012." Retrieved

March 31, 2016 (https://nces.ed.gov/surveys/sass/tables/sass1112_2013314_t1s_007.asp).

National Clearinghouse for Educational Facilities. "School Grounds." Retrieved April 5, 2016 (http://www.ncef.org/school-grounds).

Ngo, Nancy. "Got Manners? With Prom Season in Full Swing, More Teenagers Are Taking Advantage of Etiquette Classes at School and Beyond." *St. Paul Pioneer Press*.

Palo Alto Medical Foundation. "Easy Etiquette for Preteens: Minding Your Manners." Retrieved March 12, 2016 (http://www.pamf.org/preteen/growingup/etiquette.html).

Rice, E., R. Petering, H. Rhoades, et. al. "Cyberbullying Perpetration and Victimization Among Middle-School Students." *American Journal of Public Health*, March 2015.

Rossi, Patricia. *Everyday Etiquette: How to Navigate 101 Common and Uncommon Social Situations.* New York, NY: St. Martin's Griffin, 2011.

SAGE Publications. *Encyclopedia of School Health.* Los Angeles, CA: SAGE Reference, 2013.

Samek, Diana R., et al. "High School Sports Involvement Diminishes the Association Between Childhood Conduct Disorder and Adult Antisocial Behavior." *Journal of Adolescent Health*, July 2015.

Senning, Cindy Post. *Emily Posts' Prom and Party Etiquette.* New York, NY: Collins, 2010.

Suddath, Claire. "A Brief History of the Prom." *Time*, May 17, 2010. Retrieved May 16, 2016 (http://content.time.com/time/magazine/article/0,9171,1987594,00.html).

Widrich, Leo. "Which Words Matter the Most When You Talk." *Fast Company*, April 4, 2014. Retrieved May 2, 2016 (http://www.fastcompany.com/3007821/which-words-matter-most-when-you-talk).

Wisegeek.com. "What is the Difference Between Etiquette and Manners?" Retrieved April 7, 2016 (http://www.wisegeek.com/what-is-the-difference-between-etiquette-and-manners.htm).

ABOUT THE AUTHOR

Katherine Yaun has a master's degree in English and teaches ESL at a university in Florida. She is also a writer and editor and has covered many topics in her career, including education, literature, and travel. Yaun has worked for state and federal departments of education and taught English internationally. She has learned about school etiquette in these settings, as well as through her own experience as a teacher and student, and is happy to share her observations with Rosen readers.

PHOTO CREDITS